OUTSMART
YOUR BRAIN

The Insider's Guide to Life-Long Memory

Ginger Schechter, MD, Denise M. Kalos, MS,
Allison McKeany, MS, RD

BROOKLYN
WRITERS PRESS

Copyright © 2020 Ginger Schechter, MD, Denise M. Kalos, MS & Allison McKeany, MS, RD

All rights reserved.
Published in New York City by the Brooklyn Writers Press,
an imprint of the Brooklyn Writers Project, LLC.

www.brooklynwriterspress.com

The Brooklyn Writers Press supports copyright. Copyright promotes free speech, inspires creativity and encourages the sharing of ideas. Thank you for purchasing an authorized edition of this book and for complying with copyright laws by not reproducing, scanning, or distributing any part of it, in any form, without permission.

TITLE: Outsmart Your Brain, The Insider's Guide to Life-Long Memory

ISBN: 978-1-7345724-1-4 (e-book)
ISBN: 978-1-7345724-2-1 (paperback)
ISBN: 978-1-7345724-3-8 (paperback, large print)

Library of Congress Catalog Card Number: 2020903867

1st Edition

AUTHOR WEBSITE: AffirmativHealth.com

PRAISE FOR
OUTSMART YOUR BRAIN
The Insider's Guide to Life-Long Memory

Far too few people understand how critical lifestyle and dietary choices are for brain function. 'Outsmart Your Brain' is an important tool to get this information, in easy-to-understand language, into the hands of those who should know it, everyone! I recommend this to anyone interested in better cognitive function.
—Ryan R. Fortna, MD, PhD, Chief Medical/Scientific Officer, ADx Healthcare

I thought I lived healthfully, what I realized is that I didn't know enough. 'Outsmart Your Brain' brings together comprehensive recommendations for maintaining memory.
—Molly S., LPC, Patient, AffirmativHealth

'Outsmart Your Brain' empowers you with the information necessary to reduce your risk for memory loss as you age. It is perfect for those whose preference it is to bypass the science and take immediate steps towards improving cognition.
—Julius Schillinger, PhD, Gateway Learning Group

TABLE OF CONTENTS

Foreword 7
Introduction 9

Chapter 1 - Overview 11
Chapter 2 - Diet & Nutrition 15
Chapter 3 - Exercise 43
Chapter 4 - Stress Management 51
Chapter 5 - Sleep 57
Chapter 6 - Socializing 65
Chapter 7 - Brain Stimulation 69
Chapter 8 - Behavior Changes 73
Chapter 9 - Supplements 77
Chapter 10 - A Path Forward 79

Appendix 81
    I. AffirmativHealth Research 2020 83
    II. Recipes 85
    III. Exercises 89

About The Authors 102

FOREWORD

Our memories are as precious as anything we own. Traditional medicine has yet to prove effective when dealing with Alzheimer's and other types of dementia. However, there is a large volume of evidence continually being presented by independent research groups and published in journals such as *Lancet* and *PLOS Medicine*, supporting the premise that modifiable medical and lifestyle risk factors can be addressed to reduce the risk of memory loss and improve cognitive function with age.

Dealing with the social and medical issues related to cognitive impairment and understanding treatment options can be both frustrating and confusing to individuals at risk of or living with Alzheimer's disease or dementia, as well as their family members. They seek alternative, science-based treatments, as pharmaceutical options are limited to slowing progression of the disease (in some), and not a cure. They want to be empowered with sufficient information to make informed decisions with regard to treatment(s). They need the information necessary to act now, rather than waiting until cognitive impairment is too severe to address.

Other books available have taken a deep dive into the science of Alzheimer's disease and other types of dementia, but the research is complicated and the recommendations are often broad and unclear. This book is designed to deliver easy-to-understand tips and strategies focused on the maintenance of cognitive function.

Brian K. Kennedy, PhD
Chief Scientific Officer
AffirmativHealth

Director of the Centre for Healthy Ageing
Professor, Departments of Biochemistry and Physiology,
Yong Loo Lin School of Medicine
National University Singapore

Professor, Buck Institute for Research on Aging

INTRODUCTION

Every 66 seconds, someone in the United States develops Alzheimer's disease. Currently, one in three seniors die with Alzheimer's or another dementia. It is estimated that this and other dementias will cost the nation up to $1.1 trillion by 2050. Something must be done before Alzheimer's steals the memories and finances of a generation.

While there still is not a cure for Alzheimer's, scientific research has identified numerous ways to reduce your risk for developing it, slow the progression if memory loss has begun, and even improve cognitive health. An article recently published in the scientific journal *Lancet* reported that approximately 35 percent of dementia risk is related to a combination of modifiable risk factors, including midlife hypertension, midlife obesity, hearing loss, late-life depression, diabetes, physical inactivity, smoking, social isolation, and education. This research supports results from a number of other studies, including a special issue dedicated entirely to dementia in *PLOS Medicine*, which indicated that lifestyle behaviors decades before Alzheimer's diagnosis are associated with risk later in life.

AffirmativHealth has conducted extensive research on brain health, including the most recent research conducted by Dr. Brian Kennedy, Chief Scientific Officer at AffirmativHealth. Through case-study trials, Dr. Kennedy identified that each person has a unique combination of factors contributing to their cognitive decline and that by addressing each person's unique body chemistry and risk profile with a personalized therapeutic plan, we can impact their cognitive function. As new scientific research is conducted around the world, AffirmativHealth's technology is continually updated to put cutting-edge science on Alzheimer's directly into the hands of patients and their caregivers who are at risk or living with the disease.

There is HOPE in the fight against Alzheimer's disease. Our program delivers personal therapeutic plans to address your unique modifiable medical and lifestyle risk factors. We also provide education and support so you can be successful in implementing a personal therapeutic plan designed to reduce your risk for Alzheimer's disease and to improve your cognitive function.

If you or someone you know can benefit from our program, please feel free to contact us at (707) 800-2302 or visit the AffirmativHealth website to learn more.

CHAPTER 1
OVERVIEW

As life expectancy in the US increases, more and more people are being diagnosed with chronic illnesses such as heart disease, cancer, stroke, arthritis, and cognitive decline. Alzheimer's disease, first described over one hundred years ago, is the slow loss of brain function that affects memory, language, and problem solving. It is estimated that there are currently 5.5 million Americans with Alzheimer's disease, and this number is expected to grow to 13.8 million by 2050.

While research has focused on finding a single cause of Alzheimer's disease, to date there is no medical cure or single effective treatment, suggesting that there likely isn't just one cause or one solution. Instead, emerging research has shown that cognitive decline is linked to a variety of factors, including: genetics, inflammation, nutrient deficiencies, cardiovascular disease, poor blood sugar control, and hormonal imbalances. Increasing evidence supports dietary and other lifestyle changes as the most effective ways to prevent, slow, or reverse cognitive decline.

One such landmark study, called the Finnish Geriatric Intervention Study to Prevent Cognitive Impairment and Disability, or FINGER for short, evaluated whether the following impacted Alzheimer's risk in over 1,000 adults: (1) both individual and group nutritional counseling, (2) exercise, including aerobic, strength, and balance, (3) a computer-based cognitive training program, and (4) management of blood pressure, weight, blood sugar, cholesterol, and other modifiable risk factors. The results demonstrated significant improvements in the standard nutritional, physical, and cognitive activities among people in this age group.

The FINGER study is now being replicated across the globe. In addition, numerous other studies have confirmed the benefits of lifestyle interventions on cognitive health, including dietary changes, nutrition supplementation, increased physical activity, stress management, adequate sleep, cognitive training, and social engagement.

Our scientific team has reviewed the research on the factors that impact Alzheimer's risk and cognitive health to develop a comprehensive evaluation of genetic, metabolic, and lifestyle risk factors, which are used to provide a personalized program of interventions that promote optimal brain function. We regularly reevaluate the cutting-edge scientific breakthroughs and adjust our interventions as appropriate, providing you with access to the most up-to-date science on cognitive health.

Our distant ancestors primarily had APOE4 genes. The APOE4 gene is known to cause inflammation and may have promoted better healing from injuries sustained from hunting and gathering activities. As humans have lived longer and under more sanitary conditions, the APOE4 gene has been linked to chronic inflammation and chronic disease later in life, including Alzheimer's disease. In fact, people with one copy of APOE4 have a 45-percent increased risk of developing Alzheimer's disease, and those with two copies have a 50–80 percent increased risk of developing Alzheimer's disease when compared with people who have APOE2 or APOE3 versions of the gene. However, even though there may be a genetic predisposition for Alzheimer's disease, there is good evidence that lifestyle factors play a strong role in maintaining cognitive health as you age.

The earlier you can identify potential causes for cognitive decline, the earlier you can take steps to correct them and preserve your cognitive health. While the thought of making changes to your diet, exercise, or sleep routine may feel overwhelming, developing realistic goals and setting your environment up for success will help you succeed. As you start to incorporate the recommendations, keep in mind that not all of the changes need to be made at once. Start with the changes that seem the easiest and slowly incorporate those that are more challenging. As you create goals, it is important to be realistic about the changes you will be able to maintain and to ask for help as it is needed. Keep in mind the time you have available, your finances, and how your health may affect what you are able to do. For example, if you have limited time to cook, it may not be realistic to make dinner from scratch each night.

Another important part of developing goals is understanding how the changes will directly benefit you on a daily basis. Having specific benefits in mind can help you stick to a plan, even when motivation wavers.

Your environment, including your physical surroundings and the people around you, plays a large role in how successful you are at making positive changes. Your environment can affect what you eat, how often you exercise, how well you sleep, and your stress levels. Setting your environment up for success is often the most powerful way to create new healthy habits.

For example, if your home or workplace provides easy access to healthy snacks, you are more likely to eat them than if you are surrounded by sugary foods or drinks. Similarly, you are more likely to make healthy eating choices if the people around you are also eating healthy and are supportive of your goals. While you can't always manage the people around you on a daily basis, you can make it a point to spend more time around people who are supportive and motivating and limit time with people who are less supportive.

By evaluating how your current environment may affect your health and choices, you can start changing your surroundings to increase your success.

As you develop goals and new habits, it is okay if you aren't perfect. New behaviors require learning, practice, and a good support system. Having a clear understanding of what is being recommended and why it is being recommended will increase your motivation and confidence. To get started, you may also find it helpful to become involved with a class on healthy cooking, exercise, or meditation. Continue to ask questions and request help from your family, friends, and healthcare providers along the way.

As time goes on, you may find that you drift out of a healthy habit because of illness, travel, change to your environment, or even loss of interest. If this happens, reach out to your support system for help getting back on track or trying a different approach. You may also find that keeping variety in your diet, exercise program, or social contacts will keep you more engaged and motivated.

CHAPTER 2
DIET & NUTRITION

Food plays the most vital role in cognitive health, as well as in overall health. Consuming a diet of minimally processed, single-source foods that is rich in vegetables, protein, and healthy fats is the first step to supporting brain health, combined with intermittent fasting.

There are many approaches to dietary recommendations for optimal brain health, including the Mediterranean Diet, the DASH diet, the Keto Diet, the MIND Diet, and a vegan diet. Based on our extensive research, we have formulated an approach that brings together the best of all of these approaches to decrease Alzheimer's Disease risk and improve cognitive function.

One of the foundations for good health is having good digestion and a healthy microbiome, which are the healthy bacteria living in your gut. Focusing on eating foods to promote the health of your gut is the most integral part of maintaining and improving cognition. In addition, intermittent fasting is encouraged to support the breakdown and recycling of unneeded substances in your brain and body. By following the recommendations in this chapter, you will manage blood glucose levels, decrease inflammation, and improve your overall nutrient intake.

DIET FOUNDATION

The foundational components of a brain-healthy diet include:

- Prebiotic and probiotic-rich foods for microbiome health
- Non-starchy vegetables, including leafy greens, daily
- Lean protein, focusing on plant-based and fish proteins
- Healthy fats coming from plant and fish sources
- Unprocessed, gluten-free carbohydrates

DIET & NUTRITION

Probiotics & Prebiotics

The healthy bacteria living in the small intestine makes up the microbiome, which is intricately involved in health and cognition. A thriving microbiome supports digestion, immune system function, metabolism, and brain function.

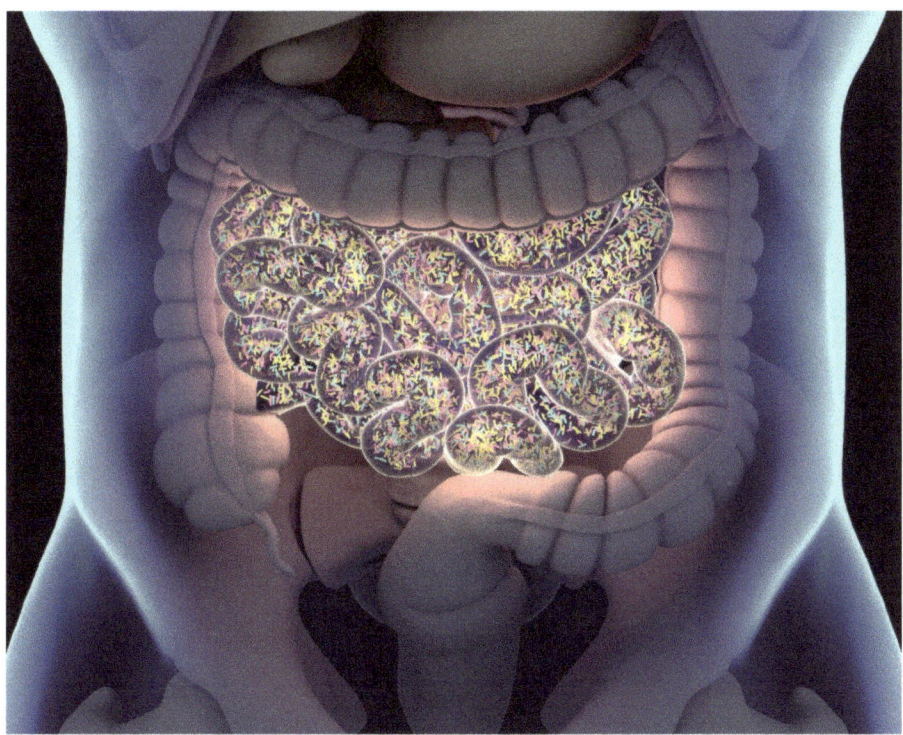

Probiotics are live bacteria that support the microbiome. Food sources of probiotics come from cultured and fermented foods, including: yogurt, kefir, kombucha, tempeh, miso, kimchi, sauerkraut, and other fermented vegetables.

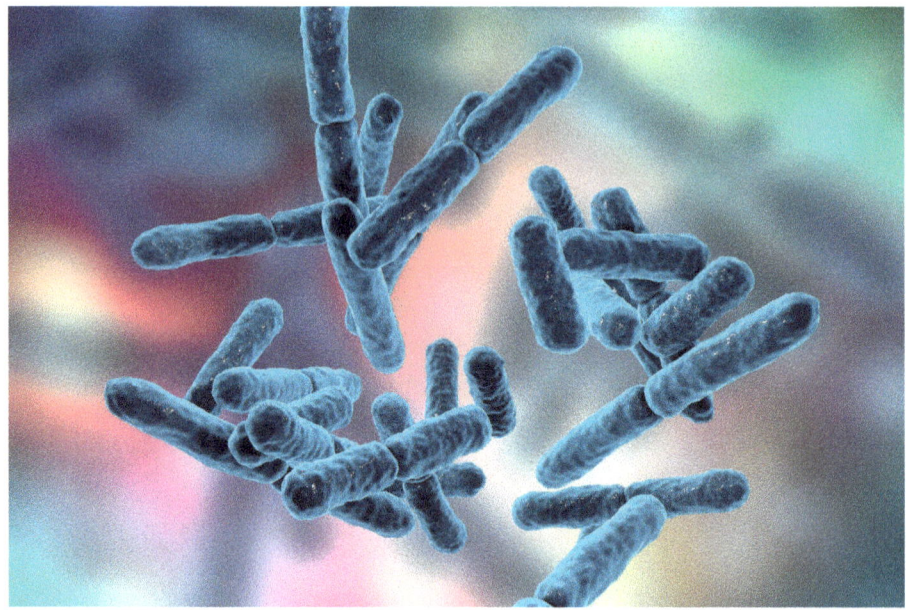

While food sources of probiotics are preferred, high-quality probiotic supplements may be taken daily. Look for probiotic supplements with *Lactobacillus acidophilus* and *Bifidobacterium lactis* with at least 4–8 billion colonies.

Prebiotics are the undigested fiber compounds in food that provide fuel for probiotics and microbiome health. Food sources of prebiotics include: flax, leafy greens, legumes, leeks, garlic, and dandelion greens. Regularly consuming beans, legumes, nuts, seeds, and non-starchy vegetables will meet probiotic needs.

Non-Starchy Vegetables

Non-starchy vegetables provide a variety of vitamins and minerals that support brain health and decrease inflammation. Non-starchy vegetables that are low in carbohydrates and high in fiber support blood sugar control and meal satiety. Many vegetables also provide prebiotics to support the health of the microbiome within the digestive system.

Non-starchy vegetables include vegetables other than corn, potatoes, peas, and winter squash, which are starchy and contribute to carbohydrate intake (see Grains & Starches section).

Focus on fresh, in-season, organic produce when available to maximize antioxidant intake and minimize toxins. When produce items are out of season, choose frozen options and limit canned, processed, and pre-seasoned products.

If organic produce options are not readily available or affordable, the Environmental Working Group (EWG) publishes a list of the fruits and vegetables that have the lowest and highest pesticide residues. Items on the "Clean 15" list can be purchased conventionally grown, and those on the "Dirty Dozen" list should be purchased organic. The list is updated annually and can be found online at the Environmental Working Group, www.ewg.org, or by downloading the "Dirty Dozen" cellphone app.

The EWG 2020 list is as follows:

The Clean 15 Food List

1. Onion
2. Avocado
3. Sweet corn
4. Pineapple
5. Asparagus
6. Sweet peas
7. Kiwi
8. Cabbage
9. Eggplant
10. Papaya
11. Watermelon
12. Broccoli
13. Cauliflower
14. Cantaloupes
15. Mushrooms

This list of foods is kept up to date each year by the nonprofit Environmental Working Group.

The Environmental Working Group also suggests a reason to buy several of the Clean 15 foods when they are organically grown. Some varieties of sweet corn, papaya, and summer squash sold in the United States are produced from genetically modified seeds. Buy organic varieties of these crops if you want to be sure to avoid genetically modified produce.

The Dirty Dozen Food List

1. Strawberries
2. Spinach
3. Kale
4. Nectarines
5. Apples
6. Grapes
7. Peaches
8. Cherries
9. Pears
10. Tomatoes
11. Celery
12. Potatoes

* The EWG also has a supplementary warning on hot peppers, which they sneak onto the list.

Have at least five ½-cup servings of vegetables per day, choosing a variety of vegetables in a variety of colors to take advantage of the array of nutrients. Incorporate leafy greens (kale, spinach, chard, kale, collards) daily and cruciferous vegetables (broccoli, cauliflower, cabbage, brussels sprouts) often. Using a variety of cooking methods can increase nutrient availability and help keep regular vegetable intake exciting and delicious.

Protein

Protein plays an important role in blood sugar stability, satiety, immune system health, and muscle maintenance. Incorporating protein foods into each meal and snack ensures adequate intake and improves blood glucose control.

Plant-based proteins are preferred, as they provide fiber and prebiotics essential for immune system support and digestive health. Animal-based proteins provide vitamin B12, iron, and brain-healthy fats and can be consumed in moderation. Avoid all processed meats, including bacon, sausage, and lunchmeat, as they contain unhealthy fats, high amounts of sodium, and disease-promoting preservatives.

ENJOY FREQUENTLY	Beans, legumes, nuts & seeds, nut butter, tofu, tempeh, fish, eggs, poultry
ENJOY OCCASIONALLY	Dairy products, grass-fed beef
AVOID	Processed meats: bacon, sausage, lunch meat

Plant-Based Proteins to Choose More Often

Beans & Legumes

Beans and legumes contain soluble and insoluble fiber as well as resistant starch, which are all important for digestive health and blood sugar regulation. Beans and legumes are also a good source of folate, a nutrient important for lowering levels of homocysteine, a risk factor for Alzheimer's disease. Beans also contain a number of other nutrients, including zinc, calcium, magnesium, and other health-promoting antioxidants and phytonutrients.

Beans and legumes have high levels of phytic acid, which decreases absorption of some nutrients. It is recommended to soak and rinse dry beans before cooking them or to use sprouted beans, such as sprouted lentils or mung beans. If canned products are more convenient, choose BPA-free cans and salt-free options and rinse before using to remove excess sodium and the gas-promoting raffinose compound. Mung beans, black-eyed peas, black beans, and lentils tend to be well-tolerated options, especially when introduced into the diet slowly, and more so if they are sprouted.

Incorporate at least a ½-cup serving of beans and legumes most days of the week by substituting beans or lentils for an animal protein source or adding to soups, salads, egg dishes, and dips.

Nuts & Seeds

Nuts and seeds contain protein, fiber, and healthy fats that support brain health by managing glucose levels and insulin. Regular nut consumption has been shown to reduce cholesterol, insulin resistance, and inflammation, as well as a number of chronic diseases. Nuts also provide a variety of vitamins and minerals, including vitamin E, selenium, potassium, zinc, and folate in addition to antioxidants and phytonutrients.

Nuts, similar to beans and legumes, contain phytic acid that decreases nutrient absorption. Consuming soaked or sprouted nuts, which can be purchased or made at home, decreases the phytic-acid content and improves digestibility.

There is early research that suggests that consuming some phytic acid may be beneficial in the treatment of Alzheimer's disease. Until more is known about the link between phytic acid and cognitive function, consume a variety of nuts, both soaked and raw, for maximum benefit.

Incorporate at least a ¼-cup serving of nuts and seeds daily by adding nuts and seeds to oatmeal, smoothies, and salads or pairing nuts or nut butters with vegetables or fruits for a filling snack. Remember: peanuts are not nuts! They are legumes!

DIET & NUTRITION

Tofu & Tempeh

Soy products, including soybeans (edamame), tofu, and tempeh (fermented soybeans), are high in protein and fiber as well as nutrients like folate, magnesium, iron, and omega-3 fatty acids. The isoflavones in soy have been shown to improve cognitive function and cardiovascular health and reduce the risk for cancer and cancer recurrence, including breast cancer.

Choose up to two servings of soy products daily, focusing on whole soy sources like soybeans, tofu, and tempeh. Limit intake of processed soy foods made with "textured soy protein (TSP)" and protein powders, which have not been shown to have the same benefits of whole soy foods.

Animal-Based Proteins to Choose in Moderation

Fish

Fish have protein and brain-healthy omega-3 fatty acids, as well as vitamin B12, which supports homocysteine metabolism. Consume one to two servings of wild-caught fish per week, focusing on cold-water fatty fish like salmon, mackerel, and herring.

As many fish contain high levels of mercury and other contaminants, avoid shark, king mackerel, swordfish, tilefish, and tuna and refer to the Environmental Working Group website (www.ewg.org) or the Environmental Protection Agency website (www.epa.gov) for more information about safe seafood choices. If tuna is an inexpensive choice, then only eat the dark meat tuna, not albacore. This is because the dark meat of the tuna has less mercury than the light or white meat.

Eggs

Eggs are a rich source of protein, choline, and cholesterol needed to optimize brain health. Choline is an important building block for the neurotransmitters needed for memory and communication. While the cholesterol in egg yolks is often a concern, consuming the equivalent of one egg yolk per day has not been shown to significantly elevate blood cholesterol levels.

Using eggs as a protein-rich breakfast can help decrease the intake of high-carbohydrate and sweetened breakfast items and can easily be paired with vegetables and healthy fats to support balanced blood sugar throughout the day. Eggs can also be used as a snack or an addition to any meal, as they are a budget-friendly protein option.

Poultry

Both chicken and turkey are sources of easily digested protein and provide important B vitamins and minerals such as zinc and iron. Moderate consumption of lean poultry has been associated with a healthier body weight, decreased risk of diabetes, and cardiovascular health.

Choose 3 to 4-ounce portions of organic, pasture-raised poultry two to three times per week. Pasture-raised poultry supplies higher amounts of omega-3 fatty acids than conventionally raised products. Poultry should be cooked to an internal temperature of 165 degrees Fahrenheit to avoid E. coli and other contamination.

DIET & NUTRITION

Animal-Based Proteins to Limit

Dairy Products

The role of dairy products and saturated fat in health remains controversial. While dairy products can be a quality protein source, many are high in saturated fats, sodium, and sweeteners. For many people, dairy proteins are difficult to digest and may be inflammatory.

If incorporating dairy products, the best options are unsweetened cultured yogurts or kefirs, which provide probiotics to support microbiome health. Use cheese and dairy milk sparingly, or try goat milk, nut milk, oat milk, or coconut milk options that are easier to digest. Most nut milks are produced with thickeners like guar gum and carrageenan. These can be pro-inflammatory and difficult to digest. The best source for nut milk is to make your own. As this may be more expensive, the best options for non-dairy "milk" are goat milk, oat milk, and coconut milk, given that these thickeners are not present in these products.

Red Meat

Red meat, including beef, lamb, pork, and other varieties, is a good source of protein, B vitamins, and iron. However, red meat has been associated with increased risk for cardiovascular disease and diabetes. Risks are even higher when processed red meats, such as bacon or sausage, are consumed.

If consuming red meat, do so sparingly. Some of the healthiest cultures in the world consume red meat products only on special occasions instead of regularly incorporating it into their diet. The best red meat sources come from grass-fed, organic animals, which provide omega-3 fatty acids, medium-chain triglycerides, and increased vitamin and mineral contents. Your best choice is to not eat beef at all if you are not able to get grass-fed options.

Healthy Fats

Adequate fat and cholesterol intake is essential for brain health and cognition. The most beneficial fats come from plant sources and include monounsaturated fats, polyunsaturated fats, and medium-chain triglycerides. Include at least one type of healthy fat with each meal. Limit intake of saturated fats from animal sources and avoid chemically formed *trans* fats, referred to as "partially hydrogenated" oils on food label ingredients lists.

Monounsaturated Fats

Found in nuts, olives, olive oil, and avocados, monounsaturated fats support cognitive health and memory, decrease inflammation, improve blood glucose control, and promote meal satiety. Olive oil is a staple of the Mediterranean diet, and regular consumption is thought to improve cholesterol profiles, decrease inflammation, and decrease risk for cardiovascular disease.

Regularly use olive oil in salad dressings and low-temperature cooking. Use avocado or grapeseed oil for high-temperature cooking and baking. Rely on a variety of nuts and nut butters made without added sugars or trans fats as healthy additions to meals or snacks. Substitute grain flour for nut-based flour in baked goods to decrease blood sugar burden.

Polyunsaturated Fats

Polyunsaturated fats, also known as omega-3 fats, are found in walnuts, flaxseeds, pumpkin seeds, sunflower oil, sesame oil, and cold-water fish. Regular intake of omega-3-rich foods decreases inflammation and can reduce the risk of many chronic diseases.

Eat ground flaxseeds and pumpkin seeds for improved digestion and absorption; add to hot cereal, smoothies, or baked goods, or use as a breading for fish or poultry. Keep pre-ground flaxseed in the refrigerator or freezer to prevent them from becoming rancid. It is important that flaxseeds be ground, or they will just pass through the body and provide no value. Incorporate walnuts frequently for snacks or with meals. Consume wild-caught cold-water fish one to two times per week.

Medium-Chain Triglycerides

Medium-chain triglycerides (MCTs) are easily digested and metabolized and support the formation of ketones, which are a fuel source for the brain. MCTs have shown promising benefits for a number of neurological disorders, including dementia and Alzheimer's disease.

Coconut oil is approximately two-thirds MCTs, making it a good source of this brain-healthy fuel. Choose organic coconut oil, either virgin or refined, made with no chemical agents. Virgin coconut oil has a more distinctive sweet and nutty coconut flavor and can be heated up to 350 degrees Fahrenheit. Refined coconut oil has a more neutral flavor and can be heated up to 400 degrees Fahrenheit. Incorporate 1 or more tablespoons of coconut oil into your diet by adding to coffee or tea, using in place of oils for cooking vegetables, eggs, or fish, or eating by the spoonful.

Ghee, made by heating butter to a high temperature to remove milk proteins and water, is two-thirds saturated fats, some of which may improve digestion, decrease inflammation, and improve the health of your microbiome. Ghee is also a source of vitamin A, vitamin E, and vitamin K. While olive oil is the preferred source of fat for brain health, ghee can be used occasionally when you are looking for a nutty, buttery flavor or need an oil with a higher smoke point. For the most health benefits, choose ghee made from grass-fed milk.

Unprocessed, Gluten-Free Carbohydrates

Carbohydrates are found in grains, anything made with grain flour, starchy vegetables, fruit, and milk. Carbohydrates are digested into glucose and move into the bloodstream, triggering a rise in insulin levels. As elevated glucose and insulin levels are risk factors for cognitive decline, limit carbohydrate servings to no more than ½–1 cup with meals. Choose minimally processed carbohydrates and limit highly processed grain and fruit products and foods made with grain flour.

Gluten-Free Grains

Gluten, a protein found in wheat, barley, and rye, has been found to cause gastrointestinal inflammation and may in some cause intestinal permeability. In the most extreme form, it causes celiac disease, which is a true allergy to gluten. The increased inflammatory response may result in increased inflammation in the brain, leading to a number of neurological symptoms including cognitive decline.

Choose "single ingredient" gluten-free grains, such as wild rice, quinoa (technically a seed), or oats labeled gluten free, limiting highly processed gluten-free products like bread, crackers, pastries, and desserts.

CHOOSE	*quinoa, brown rice, wild rice, oats, nut flours, millet, amaranth*
AVOID	*Wheat (durum, semolina, spelt, farina, faro), barley, rye, triticale, malt, Brewer's Yeast*

Starchy Vegetables

Vegetables such as potatoes, corn, peas, and winter squash are sources of carbohydrates. These are also broken down into glucose-like grains.

When consuming starchy vegetables, choose darker pigmented options like sweet potatoes or purple potatoes for increased nutrient content. Prepare starchy vegetables by roasting or sautéing instead of mashing or frying.

DIET & NUTRITION

Fruit

Fruits are great sources of fiber, vitamins, antioxidants, and phytonutrients but do contribute to carbohydrate intake and are broken down into glucose-like grains.

Berries have been shown to be especially important for brain health and memory. Try to incorporate fresh or frozen berries most days per week. When choosing other fruits, focus on lower sugar options such as apples, pears, citrus, and stone fruits. Limit high-sugar fruits like grapes, bananas, and tropical fruits. Consume fruit with protein and fat to increase satiety and improve blood sugar control.

Meal Planning

- Include protein, healthy fat, and non-starchy vegetables with each meal.

- Include protein and/or fat with each snack.

- Limit total carbohydrate intake to ½–1 cup servings of minimally processed, gluten-free options.

- Use the Plate Method for portioning out meals, with one-half plate filled with non-starchy vegetables, one-quarter plate filled with protein and healthy fats, and no more than one-quarter plate filled with carbohydrates.

Caffeine

Research is mixed about the potential benefits of caffeine on cognitive health. Research is being done to look at the effects on cognition of the active components quercetin, flavones, and chlorogenic acid found in coffee.

There is currently not enough evidence to recommend caffeine as a protective agent against cognitive decline. If consuming caffeine regularly, including hot or iced coffee or tea, consume it prior to noon to avoid sleep disruptions.

Caffeine found in chocolate may improve cognition, as chocolate intake was associated with a lower risk of cognitive decline when overall daily caffeine consumption from other sources was low. If consuming chocolate, choose products with at least 70 percent cacao to maximize cocoa intake and minimize added sugars.

INTERMITTENT FASTING

Intermittent fasting induces autophagy, which is the process that the body uses to "clean up" unneeded debris and repair itself. Autophagy is important for supporting neuronal health and for clearing beta-amyloid, a type of neural protein accumulation associated with memory loss.

Avoid calorie intake for at least 3 hours prior to bed and eat within an 8-12-hour window during the day to achieve the benefits of intermittent fasting. This eating schedule will support a 12-16 hour nightly fast to facilitate autophagy, improve blood sugar regulation, and lower body weight.

CHAPTER 3
EXERCISE

Participating in regular exercise can improve cognition, balance, and strength. Exercise lowers blood glucose and insulin levels, reduces levels of inflammation, and promotes the health and survival of brain cells. Exercise also improves mood and sleep and reduces stress and anxiety, which are all associated with cognitive health.

There are three primary forms of exercise:

1. **Aerobic** increases your heart rate and breathing rate, raises your body temperature, and strengthens your heart and lungs.

2. **Strength** activities that make muscles stronger.

3. **Balance** exercises that strengthen the muscles that help keep you upright, including your legs and core. These kinds of exercises can improve stability and help prevent falls.

AEROBIC EXERCISE

Examples of aerobic exercise include:

- Walking
- Bicycling
- Swimming
- Water aerobics
- Dancing
- Doing yard work
- Any other activity that moderately increases your breathing and heart rate and may cause you to sweat

STRENGTH TRAINING

As you age, strength training is important to maintain muscle strength and to reduce the risk for falls and broken bones. To get the most out of strength training, work different muscle groups, including your legs, hips, back, abdomen, chest, shoulders, and arms.

Examples of strength-training exercises include:

- Free weights
- Weight machines
- Resistance bands
- Or even your own body weight

The most beneficial strength-training exercises are those that mimic the activities from your daily life. When you move your body throughout the day, you use different muscle groups and move your joints in different directions. For example, when you are emptying the dishwasher, you lift and turn. When you get dressed, you bend, reach, and pull.

Therefore, when doing strength-training exercises, try to use multiple movements and multiple muscles at one time. Exercising multiple body parts at the same time can also reduce the amount of time you need to spend exercising and has the added benefit of challenging your brain to coordinate the movements. Activities like Pilates and yoga are excellent options that require strength, flexibility, balance, and thinking.

People who do both aerobic and strength exercise have improved attention and working memory compared to those who do aerobic exercise alone.

In addition to aerobic and strength training, incorporating balance activities can challenge your brain and reduce the risk of falls.

BALANCE TRAINING

Balance training can be a formal class like yoga, a video you watch at home, or a routine that you develop with a physical therapist. You can also incorporate balance exercises into daily life.

For example:

- Stand on one foot while brushing your teeth
- Walk heel to toe around your house
- Do back and side leg raises while washing the dishes

When starting a new balance activity, keep something sturdy close by so that you can steady yourself, such as a chair, the counter, or the wall. Balance is a skill, and like any other skill, regular practice is important.

Yoga is a beneficial form of exercise because it offers strength and balance training together with gentle stretching to improve flexibility.

People who regularly practice yoga have improved working memory. Yoga can also improve posture, mobility, and balance.

FIT—Frequency, Intensity, and Time

How much exercise do you need to do to gain the benefits? Exercise guidelines can be explained using the **FIT** principle, which stands for **F**requency, **I**ntensity, and **T**ime.

Frequency

Each week try to do three to five days of aerobic exercise, two non-consecutive days of strength training exercises, and at least three days of balance exercises.

Intensity

When you are doing exercise, aim to reach a moderate intensity level. Intensity level varies from person to person, due to current fitness level, medical conditions, and possible medication side effects. At a moderate intensity level, you should be able to talk comfortably or sing along with a song without difficulty or gasping for breath. Working within your own limits will allow you to reap the benefits of aerobic activity safely and enjoyably.

Time

If you are not currently exercising, it is important to begin slowly. Work up to 150 minutes, or 2 ½ hours of total aerobic exercise each week. If you are already exercising 150 minutes weekly, or when you reach that goal, increase to 300 minutes, or 5 hours each week for the greatest health benefits.

Incorporating short bursts of exercise throughout your day is also a way to get the benefits of exercise. Try parking farther away or taking the stairs instead of an elevator or escalator to add exercise minutes into your daily routine.

As you work to incorporate or increase the amount and type of exercise into your week, keep the following tips in mind to help your exercise routine become a habit:

- Whatever activities you choose, make sure they are enjoyable. Include friends and nature whenever possible and don't be afraid to try new things. Gardening, dancing, walking, biking, swimming, yoga, and so many other activities are great for your mind and body.

- You don't need fancy equipment or a gym membership to gain the benefits of exercise. Walking is a form of exercise that doesn't require anything other than a pair of shoes. In addition, many household items can be used for a variety of exercises, such as stairs, chairs, and milk jugs.

- Incorporate movement into everyday life whenever possible.

- Don't be afraid to ask for a referral to a physical therapist to guide you through appropriate exercises.

SUMMARY

Overall, for maximum cognitive and overall health benefits, try to incorporate:

- 150–300 minutes of moderate-intensity aerobic activity each week

- Strength-training exercises at least two times per week

- Balance exercises at least three times per week

And as with any exercise program, please speak with your physician about your current health status before you begin any physical training.

CHAPTER 4
STRESS MANAGEMENT

While some forms of stress may be beneficial, chronic stress can negatively affect your physical, mental, and cognitive health. Stress is the physical response you have to real or imagined change in your environment. When you experience stress, hormones are released that increase your heart rate and breathing rate as your body gets ready to either fight with the stressor or run away from it. However, most of the stressors in your life, such as your job, traffic, or bills, are not events that you can fight or run from. Without *actually* fighting or running, your body does not burn off the stress-producing hormones, which can lead to the many negative health effects of stress.

Sometimes stress can be useful, and this is called *eustress*. Short-term stress, such as when you are trying to meet a work deadline, can actually help you be more productive and does not usually cause long-term harm. *Distress* is the long-term stress response that leads to chronic stress, which may have a negative impact on your health.

Everyone reacts differently to stressors, and sometimes even positive life events, such as family gatherings, holidays, weddings, traveling, or buying a new home, can lead to chronic stress. As you become more aware of your stressors and how stress affects you, keep in mind that stress can be an opportunity for growth *or* an obstacle to your well-being. Take this time to find a form of relaxation that you can use to manage your stress.

Deep breathing, meditation, yoga, tai chi, exercise, and listening to calming music are all examples of activities that can help with stress management. The method you choose is not as important as how it makes you feel. If you find that you are frustrated by one relaxation method, try something new until you find a good fit.

Relaxation is the process of clearing your mind of worry, decreasing stress hormones, and lowering your physical response to stress. Relaxation can increase confidence, focus, and clarity, strengthen your immune system, relieve pain, and manage blood pressure and blood sugar levels.

While sitting quietly, reading a book, or watching TV are enjoyable for some people, they may not be sufficient to manage your stress.

MEDITATION

Meditation is a relaxation technique used around the world. Meditation is also beneficial for cognitive health, and patients with Alzheimer's disease and their caregivers who practiced meditation had less stress, better sleep, and improved well-being.

There are several types of meditation, including:

- Mindfulness meditation
- Movement meditation
- Progressive muscular relaxation

Mindfulness Meditation

Learning to become more mindful, which is focusing on the present moment instead of worrying about the past or present, is a way to promote relaxation. Mindfulness meditation is the most common form of meditation in the Western part of the world. To practice mindfulness meditation, sit or lie quietly and focus on the feeling of your breath coming into your nostrils and filling your abdomen. If your attention wanders, gently bring your focus back to the sensation of breathing.

Movement Meditation

Movement meditation works well for people who like to be active with their body or mind. Movement meditation activities include:

- Yoga
- Walking outdoors
- Gardening
- Qigong
- Art (coloring, painting, sculpture)

Progressive Muscular Meditation

Progressive muscular meditation is a technique where you focus on slowly tensing and then relaxing each muscle group in your body one at a time.

TIME

To gain the stress-relieving effects of meditation, meditate for at least 10 minutes per day 5 days each week.

ENVIRONMENT

Your environment plays an important role in your ability to practice relaxation:

- Schedule a relaxation break into your daily routine so that it doesn't get pushed aside. This may be as simple as taking a few deep breaths throughout the day or finding a time and place to meditate or practice a few yoga poses.

- Whatever relaxation method works for you, find a place that is calming and quiet. Being outdoors surrounded by fresh air and sunlight is relaxing for the body and the mind.

PRACTICE

Similarly to playing a sport or a musical instrument, practice is necessary for success. If you aren't currently in the routine of practicing stress management, it may take some time until it feels natural and becomes a habit. Overall, as you practice relaxation techniques, you will improve your physical and cognitive health. Even the simple act of taking a few slow, deep breaths can calm your body and mind, no matter the situation.

Remember that relaxing is not being lazy or unproductive. It is essential for your health, so give yourself permission to breathe, relax, and unwind. Your brain and body will thank you.

CHAPTER 5
SLEEP

Sleep is strongly associated with cognitive health, and poor sleep may be both a cause and a symptom of Alzheimer's disease. Many cognitive functions, including attention, memory, language, and reasoning are affected by sleep. Some studies estimate 15 percent of Alzheimer's disease may be attributed to inadequate or poor sleep.

When you sleep, your heart rate slows, your blood pressure lowers, and your body temperature decreases. Sleep is a time for the body to repair, reorganize, and maintain important connections within the brain. Toxic substances are also cleared from the brain during sleep to maintain proper cognitive function.

Sleep is critical for learning, forming memories, and saving memories into long-term storage. In fact, taking a short nap before learning something new may improve memory and recall of new information.

Both sleep quantity and sleep quality are important for proper brain function. Sleep deprivation can increase the risk for a variety of medical conditions, including poor cognitive function. Poor sleep quality is associated with faster cognitive decline and an increased risk of dementia.

Most adults function best with 8 hours of sleep per night. However, getting adequate sleep is not always easy and the ability to sleep 7 to 8 hours at one time may decline with age. Approximately 25 percent of US adults report inadequate sleep.

Signs of inadequate and poor sleep vary from person to person, but may include the following:

- Feeling tired when you wake up
- Regularly feeling tired throughout the day
- Relying on caffeine to make it through the day
- Frequently "sleeping in" on the weekends
- Having difficulty with focus, concentration, or memory
- Falling asleep immediately at night
- Getting sick often
- Regularly experiencing depression or anxiety
- Morning headaches

Inadequate or irregular sleep may be caused by medical conditions such as arthritis or chronic pain, which may make it difficult to fall asleep or stay asleep. In addition, certain medications can disrupt sleep.

Sleep-related disorders, such as insomnia, restless leg syndrome, and sleep apnea, may also cause inadequate or irregular sleep.

SLEEP APNEA

While sleep apnea is about as common as diabetes and asthma, only a fraction of patients have been diagnosed and treated. Sleep apnea is a disorder where you have one or more pauses in breathing or shallow breathing while you sleep. These pauses in breathing may last for a few seconds or up to a few minutes and may happen as often as thirty or more times per hour. This increases the risk for stroke, heart disease, and cognitive decline.

Speak to your doctor about being evaluated for sleep apnea if you snore, wake up with a dry throat, or are tired during the day after what you thought was a good night's sleep.

SLEEP ENVIRONMENT

Your body has an internal clock, called your circadian rhythm, that uses body temperature and hormones to make you feel sleepy or alert at different times of the day. Understanding what your body needs to support your circadian rhythm can help you create a sleep environment and sleep routine that improve your quantity and quality of sleep.

Body temperature affects your circadian rhythm. As it becomes darker and bedtime nears, your body temperature will rise and you will become sleepy. This is why taking a bath before bed may help you get to sleep. Throughout the night, your body temperature decreases and then begins to increase again once morning nears.

Sleeping in an environment that is too warm, too cold, or too humid can disrupt your sleep. The ideal bedroom temperature is 65 degrees Fahrenheit.

Light can also affect your circadian rhythm. When you are surrounded by sources of light, you will be more alert. However, as it gets darker, your body produces a hormone called melatonin, which makes you feel drowsy. Artificial light coming from house lights, television, or computer or cellphone screens can confuse your circadian rhythm and make it difficult to fall asleep or stay asleep.

Sleep is also affected by your senses, as certain smells and sounds may affect your sleep. For example, the scent of lavender may promote relaxation and improve quality of sleep. Soothing sounds such as calming music, guided imagery, nature sounds, or white noise can help you relax before bed or if you wake in the middle of the night.

Finally, your emotions can affect your quality of sleep. If you are feeling stressed, anxious, upset, or worried, you will have more difficulty falling and staying asleep.

BEDROOM

You can design your bedroom environment to promote the proper temperature, light, and relaxation:

- Choose bedding that is soft and breathable, such as cotton or bamboo. While thread count may impact the feel and durability of your sheets, it is most important that they feel good to your touch. You may choose to have lighter-weight sheets in the summer and heavier sheets, such as flannel, in the winter.

- It may be helpful to use a fan or open windows in the summer months to keep your room cool.

- Choose pajamas that are light and breathable, such as cotton.

- Use dark shades or blackout blinds to minimize stimulating outside light.

- Lower the lighting in your room by using a lower-wattage light bulb or a dimmer switch.

- Avoid blue lights from electronics for at least 1–2 hours before bed.

- Use lavender essential oils in a bath, sprayed on your pillow, or throughout your bedroom.

- While waking up without an alarm clock is preferred, there are options that use soft lights or peaceful sounds to gently wake you up if needed.

- Keep your bedroom free of clutter, piles of laundry, and paperwork to promote relaxation and sleep.

- Use your bedroom for sleep and romance only. Try to avoid working, doing chores, using electronics, or engaging in other stimulating activities where you sleep.

- Choose bedroom colors that are soothing blues or greens instead of stimulating reds, yellows, oranges, or purples.

BEDTIME ROUTINE

In addition to developing an environment to promote sleep, establishing a routine can prepare your body and improve sleep quantity and quality:

- Go to bed and get up at about the same time each day. If you feel like you need to "sleep in" on the weekends or rely on an alarm clock, you likely aren't getting enough sleep.

- Try to have exposure to sunlight every day, which can help support your circadian rhythm.

- Limit naps to no more than 30 minutes during the day. Napping does not make up for missed sleep and may affect your ability to sleep at night.

- Limit caffeine intake to 1–2 cups of coffee or tea consumed before noon, as it takes about 6 hours for half of the caffeine to be eliminated from your body. Caffeine is a stimulant that increases energy and alertness and decreases sleep-producing chemicals. Caffeine is most commonly found in tea, coffee, chocolate, cocoa, soft drinks, medicines, and supplements. If you are experiencing insomnia, you may want to try eliminating caffeine entirely.

- Eating foods high in tryptophan, calcium, magnesium, or melatonin, such as walnuts, almonds, lettuce and leafy greens, fish, or dairy products, may improve sleep. Drinking chamomile tea before bed can also help promote relaxation and sleep.

- Finish your last meal at least 3 hours before you go to bed to improve digestion and sleep. Eating larger meals earlier in the day and lighter meals later in the day can also improve sleep quality.

- Refrain from drinking alcohol before bed. While alcohol may help some people fall asleep, consuming alcohol before bed can actually prevent deep sleep.

- While exercise is important for cognitive health and can improve sleep quality, try to exercise earlier in the day so that you have time to relax prior to bed. Yoga or other stretching exercises may be calming closer to bed.

- Try meditation, light stretching, massage, or soothing music to relax 1–2 hours before bed.

- Move pets out of the bedroom before you fall asleep. Fifty-three percent of people who sleep with their pets report disturbed sleep.

- Avoid smoking, as tobacco is a stimulant that can disrupt your natural sleep-wake cycle. People who smoke are more likely to suffer from sleep apnea, insomnia, and more restless sleep.

If you continue to struggle with getting adequate sleep despite a soothing environment and bedtime routine, speak with your doctor to see if using a melatonin supplement or Bright Light Therapy is right for you. Bright Light Therapy is a special box that mimics outdoor light and supports your circadian rhythm.

In addition, speak with your doctor about medications or supplements that may disrupt sleep, such as asthma medications, blood pressure medications, pain relievers, antidepressants, decongestants, ginseng, or vitamin B12. Please keep in mind that stopping or altering a medication dose is never recommended without the supervision of your treating physician.

With this information, you are well on your way to a good night's sleep.

CHAPTER 6
SOCIALIZING

The value of socializing and making strong social connections with friends and family is often underappreciated. However, making and keeping good social connections may improve your cognitive health. One study found that being social in older age can reduce the risk of developing dementia by as much as 70 percent.

While being social comes easily for some people, it may be more challenging for others, especially when there are changes to health or memory. Some people may socially isolate themselves because of fear, reluctance to discuss their health concerns, boredom, hearing loss, or difficulty participating in conversations. Caregivers often experience these same feelings as well.

However, staying engaged with others in conversation is a great way to challenge your brain because it requires focus and attention. The more time you spend interacting socially, the more challenged your brain will be. A challenged brain can help prevent cognitive decline.

There are a lot of ways to have regular social connections:

- Broaden your social circle by joining a group of some kind, or if you belong to an organization you enjoy, try finding a way to get more involved.

- Religious organizations often have discussion, social, and volunteer groups.

- Book clubs are a great way to challenge your brain to think about what you've read and participate in engaging conversation with other people.

- Taking a class at a local community college or community center can be a great way to meet people and challenge your brain by learning something new. Find a class that interests you, such as photography, pottery, art, quilting, knitting, computer skills, or others.

- Join a walking club or fitness class, which can blend the benefits of social interaction and exercise. You are much more likely to stick to a fitness routine if you do it with other people.

- Craft groups are a great way to meet other people and work on an activity that challenges your brain. Community and senior centers often offer woodworking, welding, knitting, quilting, gardening, photography, cake decorating, scrapbooking, and a variety of other groups.

- Volunteering is a great way to increase social connections. Consider reaching out to your local hospital, school district, or local or national nonprofits to see how you can get more involved. Local newspapers can also be a good resource to find volunteer opportunities.

While interacting with people in person is the most ideal, engaging in virtual friendships through blog forums or social media is better than no interaction at all. Online support groups can be very helpful and may be a way to ease into more social situations.

Interacting with people isn't the only way to improve your cognition. Caring for an animal stimulates your mind and provides a sense of companionship and purpose. Owning a pet has been associated with lower rates of depression and anxiety, decreased blood pressure, and increased longevity. Pet owners also tend to be more physically active. It has even been reported that for seniors with memory loss, pets help in accessing memories from long ago.

Overall, staying socially connected is important for many aspects of health, including cognitive health. And getting more involved with your friends, family, and community is likely to be rewarding in more ways than one.

CHAPTER 7
BRAIN STIMULATION

Your brain is an amazing organ, and throughout your life it makes new pathways. The ability of the brain to make new connections is called "neuroplasticity," and this happens whenever you experience or learn something new.

It was once thought that the brain stopped growing and changing after childhood, but we now understand that this is false. New research has shown that the brain continues to change and adapt to new information throughout one's lifespan.

Throughout your life it is important to continue to learn and challenge your brain with new information in order to make as many pathways in your brain that you can. This is known as building up "cognitive reserve." The more connections and pathways you have, the more you can prevent or slow memory decline as you age.

In fact, people with more years of education, those who speak more than one language, or those who play a musical instrument have a lower risk of Alzheimer's disease. This is likely because their brains have been more challenged, have more pathways, and thus have a higher cognitive reserve.

In a study comparing the brains of taxi drivers and bus drivers in London, it was found that certain areas of the brain were larger in the taxi drivers. Why would this be? The taxi drivers had the daily challenge of navigating different routes, whereas the bus drivers typically drove a set route. Thus, the taxi drivers had created more brain connections and built up more cognitive reserve.

To build up cognitive reserve, the brain needs to be challenged in different ways. Activities that support deep thinking or problem solving include:

- Reading

- Discussion groups

- Doing puzzles

- Playing cards or board games

- Playing a musical instrument

- Learning a new language

There are many online brain-training applications and websites. While one or two of these have been shown to increase cognitive reserve, the recommendations we have made are more likely to produce long-term changes to your brain and retain more cognitive reserve.

In addition to thinking and learning new information, the brain is challenged when more senses are stimulated. When the eyes see, ears hear, tongue tastes, nose smells, or skin touches, the information is transferred to the brain to create new connections.

How can you start using this information today?

- Routine leads to a dull brain, so try to do something different—and fun—every day.

- Choose different types of activities that become increasingly more difficult over time. If you are someone who is doing a daily activity that is now easy for you, now is the time to change it up.

- Reaching "optimal frustration" is the goal. This is the point at which you are challenged but remain motivated instead of becoming overly frustrated and giving up.

Try:

- Traveling to a new place

- Taking a new route home

- Joining a book club

- Getting involved in a new sport or fitness class

- Taking a dance class

- Working on a puzzle

- Learning a new game

- Using the computer

- Taking a music, art, cooking, or craft class

- Experiencing art or theater events

- Using your non-dominant hand to do everyday tasks

- Listening to different types of music or learning the words to new songs

There are a variety of activities that you can do to challenge your brain and decrease your risk of dementia. The more often you can challenge yourself with new activities, the greater you will reduce your risk. In fact, while participation in one activity one day per week has been associated with a 7-percent reduction in the risk of dementia, participation in more activities more often was associated with a 63 percent lower risk, so the more you can do, the better off your brain will be. Ultimately, everything we have discussed in this book is an example of an activity that can add to your cognitive reserve.

CHAPTER 8
BEHAVIOR CHANGES

The tips and tools we have reviewed all require us to change behaviors or patterns of behavior that we have developed over our lifetime. While the thought of making changes to your diet, exercise, or sleep routine may feel overwhelming, developing realistic goals and setting your environment up for success will help you succeed.

Keep in mind that not all of the changes need to be made at once. Start with the changes that seem the easiest and slowly incorporate those that are more challenging.

GOALS

As you create goals, it is important to be realistic about the changes you will be able to maintain and to ask for help as is needed. Keep in mind the time you have available, your finances, and how your health may affect what you are able to do. For example, if you have limited time to cook, it may not be realistic to make dinner from scratch each night. If this is the case, you can work with a dietician or coach to discuss how meal preparation shortcuts or appropriate ready-made foods can be a more realistic way to maintain an appropriate diet. Additionally, if finances are a concern, you may opt to walk for exercise instead of joining an expensive gym. The good news is there are many different ways to incorporate the recommendations from this book.

Another important part of developing goals is understanding how the changes will directly benefit you on a daily basis. Having specific benefits in mind can help you stick to a plan, even when motivation wavers. For example, you may be motivated to exercise regularly so you have the strength to take your grandchildren to the park, or you may be motivated to make sleep a priority so you have more energy to be social during the day.

ENVIRONMENT

Your environment, including your physical surroundings and the people around you, plays a large role in how successful you are at making positive changes. Your environment can affect what you eat, how often you exercise, how well you sleep, and your stress levels. Setting your environment up for success is often the most powerful way to start making new healthy habits.

For example, if your home or workplace provides easy access to healthy snacks, you are more likely to eat them than if you are surrounded by sugary foods or drinks. Similarly, you are more likely to make healthy eating choices if the people around you are also eating healthy and are supportive of your goals. While you can't always manage the people around you on a daily basis, you can make it a point to spend more time around people who are supportive and motivating and limit time with people who are less supportive.

By evaluating how your current environment may affect your health and choices, you can start to make changes to your surroundings to increase your success.

NEW HABITS

As you develop goals and new habits, it is okay if you aren't perfect. New behaviors require learning, practice, and a good support system. Having a clear understanding of what is being recommended and why it is being recommended will increase your motivation and confidence. You may also find it helpful to get involved with a class about healthy cooking, exercise, or meditation to get you started. Many of these classes can be accessed at local community centers or through your local Parks and Recreation, which help to keep costs down. Continue to ask questions and request help from your family, friends, and healthcare providers along the way.

As time goes on, you may find that you drift out of healthy habits because of illness, travel, change to your environment, or even loss of interest. If this happens, use your support system, including friends, family, neighbors, or your healthcare providers, to help you get back on track. You may also find that keeping variety in your diet, exercise program, or social activities will keep you more engaged and motivated.

Keep in mind it took you years to develop the habits you have now. It will take time to develop new habits and make them stick. Be gentle and compassionate with yourself, knowing that each new habit helps you maintain your memory and cognition. Frustration will be part of the process and is part of the answer. Be curious about what is frustrating and why. This, in itself, can lead to improved cognition. Use it to your benefit.

CHAPTER 9
SUPPLEMENTS

While it is always best to get nutrition from food, there is a large body of research available regarding supplements and their effect on the brain and aging. There are both herbs and vitamins that can be helpful for cognition, yet this is truly where a one-size-fits-one approach is crucial. Random ingestion of certain supplements touted to improve memory or help reverse cognitive decline has not been shown to truly prevent or reverse memory loss. Specific herbs and supplements meant to address a person's unique supplement deficiencies have been shown to be helpful. That said, herbs and supplements need to be closely monitored by a healthcare practitioner, as they can be toxic if taken incorrectly or combined with prescription medication. Therefore, we do not make any recommendations for any specific supplements.

CHAPTER 10
A PATH FORWARD

Our memory is precious and truly makes us who we are. Since we are now living longer, we tend to assume the increasing prevalence of memory-related issues is a natural consequence of aging. When asked about one's biggest fear as we age, for many, memory loss is at the top of the list. To be clear, memory loss is not a predetermined risk of getting older.

Age is not a disease or a condition, and your memory is not something that should diminish with age. This book is designed to provide a path for keeping your memories intact as you age, allowing you to continue to develop new memories and helping you maintain your ability to think on your feet.

By providing you with these easy-to-learn-and-apply tips and tools, we aim to empower you with the knowledge necessary to take control of your cognitive health as you age. Our purpose in writing this book is to give each reader not only a path forward toward lasting memories but to let you know there is hope.

It is never too early to apply what we have provided in this book. Everyone wants to have a good memory, and this is possible. Applying these tips and tricks at any age will help to maintain and improve your memory.

Remember, change takes time and can be frustrating. Use this frustration to your benefit. There is a point of "optimal frustration" when the brain goes into overdrive and allows us to more effectively solve problems. Learning new things, even if they frustrate you, develops new neural connections and increases our neuroplasticity.

If you are concerned that you are at genetic risk or experiencing early stage memory loss, you are not alone. A more aggressive, personalized approach may be necessary to achieve long-term results. AffirmativHealth is here to help.

APPENDIX

AFFIRMATIVHEALTH RESEARCH - 2020
A Comprehensive Multi-Model Strategy to Mitigate Alzheimer's Disease Risk Factors Improves Aspects of Metabolism and Offsets Cognitive Decline in Individuals with Cognitive Impairment

Ginger Schechter, Gajendra Kumar Azad, Rammohan Rao, Allison McKeany, Matthew Matulaitis, Denise M. Kalos, and Brian K. Kennedy

Alzheimer's disease (AD), a chronic condition that progresses over time and is characterized by memory loss, dementia, behavioral and metabolic changes, has been extensively studied. While several therapeutic approaches have been developed, none have substantially altered disease progression. One explanation is that the disease is multifactorial in nature. Consistently, AD onset is influenced by a range of genetic and lifestyle-associated risk factors. Using the AffirmativHealth Personal Therapeutic Program, we sought to determine whether a comprehensive and personalized program, designed to mitigate risk factors of AD, could improve cognitive and metabolic function in individuals diagnosed with subjective cognitive impairment (SCI), mild cognitive impairment (MCI), and early stage AD.

Our findings in this pilot study provide evidence that a comprehensive and personalized approach designed to mitigate AD risk factors can improve risk-factor scores and stabilize cognitive function, warranting more extensive clinical study.

This study is currently under peer review for publication.

RECIPES

Simple Salad Dressing

Ingredients:

- 1 cup extra virgin olive oil
- 1/3 cup vinegar, such as balsamic, white wine, apple cider, or any other flavored vinegar (without added sugars)
- 1-2 Tbsp Dijon mustard
- Pinch of sea salt
- Pinch of ground black pepper
- Optional additions:
    - 1-2 tsp finely chopped garlic
    - 1 tsp dried herbs, such as basil, oregano, or mixed Italian herbs
    - 1 Tbsp fresh herbs
    - 1-2 tsp honey or maple syrup, to taste

Directions:

Add all ingredients to a jar with a tightly closing lid and shake until well combined.

Lemon Poppy Seed Muffins

Ingredients:

- 2 cups almond flour
- ½ tsp baking soda
- 2 Tbsp poppy seeds
- Zest of 1 lemon
- Juice of 1 lemon
- 4 large eggs
- ¼ cup honey

Directions:

1. Preheat oven to 350 degrees Fahrenheit.

2. Line standard-sized muffin tin with 8 silicone or paper muffin cups.

3. In a large bowl, combine almond flour, baking soda, poppy seeds, and lemon zest.

4. In a separate bowl, whisk together lemon juice, eggs, and honey.

5. Add egg mixture to almond flour mixture and mix together until fully incorporated.

6. Divide batter between 8 muffin cups and bake for 20-22 minutes or until toothpick inserted in the center of the muffins come out clean.

Smoothie

Ingredients:

- 1 cup full-fat plain yogurt (choose Greek-style for the most protein)
- ½ cup fresh or frozen fruit—blueberries are the best option
- Large handful, ~½ cup, greens such as spinach, chard, kale, etc.
- Optional brain-boosting additions:
    - 1-2 Tbsp chia seeds
    - 1-2 Tbsp ground flax seeds
    - 1-2 Tbsp coconut oil
    - ¼ –½ avocado
    - 1-2 Tbsp unsweetened nut butter such as almond, cashew, walnut
- Honey or maple syrup to taste, if needed

Directions:

1. Add ingredients to blender or food processor and blend until combined, scrape the sides, and blend again.

2. Freeze any leftovers in silicone popsicle molds for a healthy treat.

EXERCISE AND STRESS MANAGEMENT

Balance

Find your balance: Stand tall with your feet hip width apart. With shoulders relaxed, notice the pressure in the feet. If possible, close your eyes and sway forward and back, and side to side. Notice your body adjusting with the movement.

One leg balance: Holding on to a chair or leaning against a wall, balance on one leg lifting the other foot. Eventually bringing the knee higher. Keep your eyes focused on a stationary point in front of you. Start slow paying attention the foot pressure on the standing leg. Switch legs.

EXERCISE AND STRESS MANAGEMENT

Side stretch: Start with a side stretch taking three deep breaths. Change sides.

Stress Management

Sit comfortably, sitting straight up in a chair on a cushion on the floor. Practice taking deep belly breaths in and out through the nose. If mouth breathing is necessary, then purse the lips to regulate and slow airflow. Imagine the belly inflating like a balloon. When exhaling, draw the navel in towards the spine. Repeat three to five times.

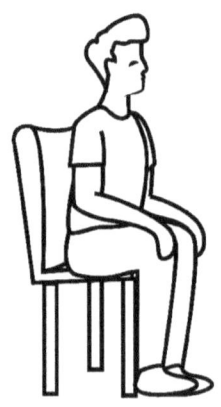

Mobility

Cat-Cow: While sitting, place your hands on your knees. When inhaling arch the lower part of your back while pressing your chest out looking upward. Exhale and round your back, bringing your chin to your chest. Repeat 3-6 times.

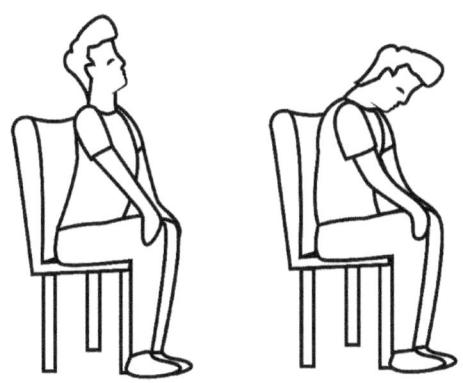

Arm reach: While sitting, inhale reaching your arms high overhead. Exhale pressing your palms out to the side as you lower your arms down to your sides. To increase difficulty, scoot your seat out to the edge of your chair. Repeat three to six times.

Chair twist: While sitting, inhale with arms above your head and exhale twisting to the right. Bring your left hand to your right knee as you bring your right elbow behind the chair. Deepen the twist while exhaling. Repeat on the other side. Repeat three to six times on each side.

OUTSMART YOUR BRAIN

Bend and twist: While sitting, spread your knees wide placing your hands on your knees. Inhale while sitting straight up on chair. Exhale bending forward bringing your right shoulder toward your left knee. Sit up and switch sides. Repeat three to six times on each side.

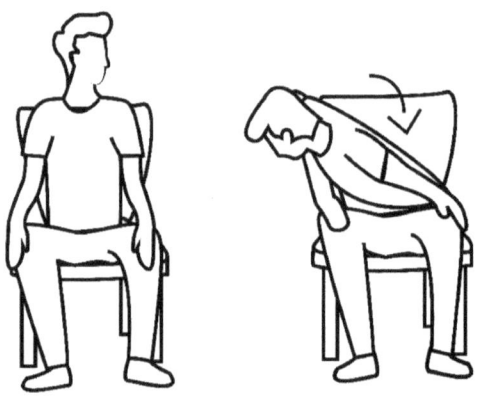

EXERCISE AND STRESS MANAGEMENT

Core strengthening: While sitting, place hands on the seat of your chair. Push through your palms and lift your bottom off the chair. Hold for five to ten seconds. Repeat three to six times.

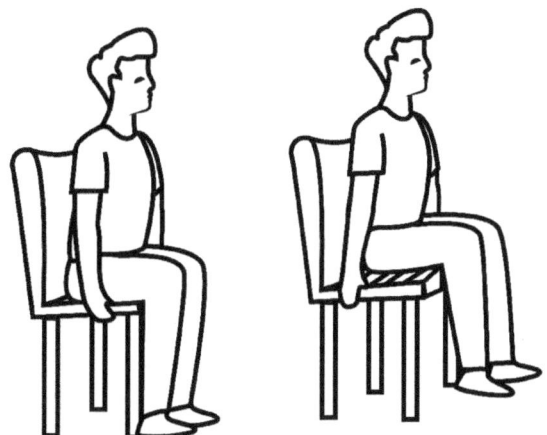

Hip opener: While sitting, place your right foot over your left knee. Place your hands on your shin and bend forward at the hips, keeping your back straight. To increase difficulty, place your elbows on your knees instead of your hands. Take five deep breaths. Sit up straight and switch sides.

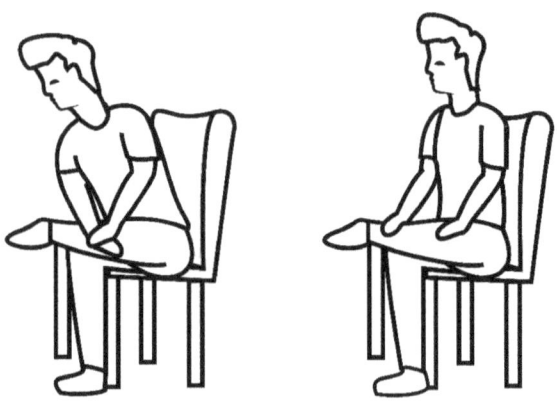

AffirmativHealth's technology is continually updated to put cutting-edge science on Alzheimer's directly into the hands of patients and their caregivers who are at risk or living with the disease. We also provide education and support so you can be successful in implementing a personal therapeutic plan designed to reduce your risk for Alzheimer's disease and to improve your cognitive function.

If you or someone you know can benefit from our program, please feel free to contact us at (707) 800-2302 or visit the AffirmativHealth website to learn more.

ABOUT THE AUTHORS

Ginger Schechter, MD

Dr. Schechter is a board-certified internal medicine physician and student of Ayurvedic medicine. Her work with the Veterans Administration as a physician and administrator offered her a unique understanding of the connection between the mind, body, and spirit specific to each patient. Throughout her career, she has always been a proponent of the role of diet and gut health as being the foundation to health and wellness. Her current position as Chief Medical Officer of AffirmativHealth allows her to continue her life's work of aligning eastern and western medicine philosophies to improve patient health. Born and raised in California, Dr. Schechter is married with two sons and a cat and is currently learning to play the ukulele.

Allison McKeany, MS, RD

Ms. McKeany is a registered dietitian and studied at University of California, San Diego. She takes a personalized approach to improving health and wellness through nutrition and lifestyle changes. Allison currently serves as the Director of Program Development for ADx Healthcare and has been partnering with AffirmativHealth since its inception. She is a key player as AffirmativHealth conducts ongoing research. Allison grew up in Sonoma, California, and enjoys the riches of wine country without ever taking a sip.

ABOUT THE AUTHORS

Denise M. Kalos, MS

Ms. Kalos is a thought leader, building wellness-related businesses, leveraging cutting edge technologies. As the Vice President of Wellbeing Programs for the Buck Institute for Research on Aging, she created the first ever program empowering people to reduce risk of memory loss and improve cognitive health. As the CEO of AffirmativHealth, she continues to raise awareness around alternative, precision therapies for those at risk or living with memory loss/Alzheimer's disease. Denise is a native San Franciscan and has never been to Alcatraz.

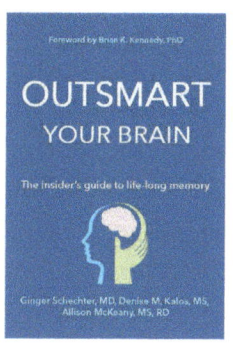

THANK YOU FOR READING
OUTSMART YOUR BRAIN
The Insider's Guide to Life-Long Memory

If you enjoyed this book, please consider leaving
a short review on Goodreads or your website of choice.

Reviews help both readers and writers.
They are an easy way to support good work and
help to encourage the continued release of quality content.

Want the latest from the Brooklyn Writers Press?
Browse our complete catalog.

www.brooklynwriterspress.com

www.ingramcontent.com/pod-product-compliance
Lightning Source LLC
Chambersburg PA
CBHW040510110526
44587CB00045B/4215